Beyond Repair and Under Construction: Seasons of a Teen

Books Coming Soon:

How to Deal with Teens who are Under Construction

What You Didn't See in the Dark

Please visit: Kerra's Comfort for more information
www.kerrascomfort.com

Beyond Repair and Closed for Construction:
Seasons of a Teen

Kerra N. Williams, M.S.

Kerra's Comfort

Copyright © 2011 by Kerra N. Williams

Published in the United States by: Kerra's Comfort
Distributed in the United States by: Kerra's Comfort: www.kerrascomfort.com. Send inquiries to:

Kerra's Comfort
P.O. Box 474
Decatur, IL 62525-0474

Library of Congress Cataloging-in-Publication Data

Williams, Kerra N: Beyond Repair and Under Construction: Seasons of a Teen/Kerra N. Williams

2011914629

ISBN: 978-0-615-52465-8

Kerra's Comfort

Printed in the United States of America

This book is dedicated to all the young people who reached out to me and touched my life in ways they will never know.

Table of Contents

<u>Acknowledgements</u>

First of all I would like to thank God for giving me a gift and allowing me to share it with the world; without God none of this would be possible and I would not exist. My first thank you goes to Tommy, my husband, my supporter, and my better half. Tommy you have been a rock for me in good and in bad times; without your constant pushing and encouraging this book would have still been in the works. Thank you for your patience, guidance, and understanding throughout this process and in our marriage. I love you and I am forever grateful.

I want to thank my mom Benita Harris for instilling in me great values and for being an excellent role model of what a woman should be. I know I have put you through a lot but believe me I have learned from the lessons you were trying to teach me and because of you I am where I am today. I love you dearly and don't you ever forget that. Keep striving for your dreams and know that I am so proud of you. To my father Robert Thompson thank you for your words of encouragement on those days where I doubted myself. You always knew that I could accomplish anything and you have always been proud of me even when I wasn't proud of myself. I love you more than you know.

To my siblings Alexis Brown, Kendra Wilson, and Kenan Thompson know that I love you more than anything and that I am so proud of you. I hope I can always make you proud and be a great example for you.

To my Aunt Kaye Thompson who has always been a phone call away and inspires me to help others. Your heart is so big and the fact that you would give others the shirt off your back speaks volumes. Thank you for always being there when I needed to talk and for putting me in my place when I needed it. I always knew you were rooting for me and wanted me to succeed!

Thanks to all my family and friends who have always supported me. All of the seeds you have planted are starting to grow and I am so grateful. Thank you to all the young people that I have come in contact with at Boys and Girls Club, Girls and Boys Town, and Teen Challenge. You guys are my inspiration for this book and know that each and every one of you has touched my life and my heart!

Introduction

"It's up to you to be happy, it's up to you to be great, it's up to you to fulfill your destiny, and it's up to you to be all that God created you to be"

-Kerra N. Williams

I know what you are thinking this is one of those "self-help" books trying to tell you how to be happy and how to have a great life. Well you're right it is that kind of book but I promise it is not as cheesy. If you don't like the first couple of chapters you can stop reading it. My feelings won't be hurt well maybe a little. I promise you that if you love them you will not want to put this book down. *Beyond Repair and Under Construction: Seasons of a Teen* is about the many transformations and struggles that teens go through on a daily basis. You can overcome anything with a little love and guidance on how to deal with anything that comes your way. Every season the weather changes and something new happens all around you and every season in your life is exactly the same. As you get older the seasons will always change and so will you. It is up to you whether you change for the better or for the worst.

Working with kids I have found that they feel like they do not have a voice and that is something that needs to change. You are **IMPORTANT**, you are **WORTH IT**, and you do have a **PURPOSE**. In today's society, there is so much pressure to be something that you're not. Either you are too skinny, not skinny enough, too smart, too dumb, too quiet, or too loud, the list can go on. It is so hard to be yourself because you want to be accepted and loved by those around you. Well I encourage you to step outside of the box and be different and set yourself apart from the rest. It is so easy to be like everybody else but it takes heart to be different.

You have a say in your life and it is up to you to want to change it. I am going to leave you with one last phrase, "If you keep doing the same things you will continue to get the same results." So, try something different. You are going to continue to make mistakes as you go through life so it is important to remember that it's what you learn from those mistakes that really matter. It is up to you to decide how you want to navigate through your seasons and since you have already decided or someone has decided for you to read this book I know you will be fine. So sit back, relax, and get lost in the seasons!

14

Winter

January
Real Talk

"Choices"

    Asia was a 15 year old girl full of promise. Asia was 5"9", slim, and was considered what some would call a tomboy. She would rather wear sweats and a t-shirt instead of wearing some tight jeans and a fitted shirt because she hated people looking at her shape. Asia played basketball and softball so she had a nice shape but was still self-conscious about the way she looked. Even though she spent a lot of time on the court and the field she made excellent grades. Everyone in the school liked her and she loved the attention. She was who everybody wanted her to be. Every year her friends would throw a party but this one was a little different.

    She noticed that a lot of the older kids came this year which made her nervous because she knew that something was going to go down. Asia had heard stories of the juniors and seniors partying too hard and people getting caught up in a lot of drama. The year before a couple of kids got arrested for fighting and a girl got so wasted that she let people take pictures of her naked. The pictures were on Facebook the next day and the girl ended up moving to another state. Even though she was nervous she did not want to look like a punk so she tried to act hard to fit in. Something told her to go home but she did not want to miss anything or seem scared.

    She saw a couple of girls popping pills and they asked if she wanted some. She knew that she should say no but how would that make her look. She asked what kind of pills they were and they all started laughing at her. Asia felt embarrassed so she grabbed a handful of them and swallowed them. At first she stood there in shock by what she just did but then she started to feel

17

like she was on cloud nine and soon became the life of the party. What she didn't know was that mixing all those pills was toxic and something bad was going to happen. Asia started dancing with a group of guys and getting a little wild and one of her friends pulled her away before it got out of hand. She didn't want Asia to do something that she would regret later. Her friend knew that Asia was getting crazy so she decided to drive her home. She walked Asia up to her room and decided that she looked fine so she left. Her friend told Asia's mom that she got sick from the food at the party and took some medicine that made her feel funny. Asia's mom thanked her friend for bringing her home and reassured her that she would take over and make sure she gets better. When Asia's mom got up to her room Asia was already lying in bed knocked out. Her mom kissed her on the cheek, whispered good night, and closed the door.

In the morning her mom walked through the door to get her up for practice but she did not budge. Her mom got angry as she continued to call her name because she knew Asia was not a morning person and usually she had to drag her out of bed. So, it was not unusual for Asia to lay there and not move. Frustrated to the point of no return her mom pulled the cover back and was horrified by what she saw. She knew immediately that something was wrong and called the ambulance. She knew it was too late and that her daughter was dead.

The mom called her friend from last night and asked her, "What medicine did Asia take?" The friend hurried up and tried to make up something random and said, "Benadryl". "Don't lie to me she is not waking up and I think she is dead." The phone went silent and all you could hear was silence on both ends of the line. When the ambulance arrived they confirmed that Asia was dead and that they would know more when they took her to the hospital. After several days the mother had been informed that her daughter had overdosed. Everyone was shocked because of the reputation Asia had and how much she had going for herself. Asia's friend finally confessed to Asia's mom that she took a hand full of pills but didn't think she would die. "People take pills all the time and nothing like this has ever happened." Asia's Mom looked at her with tears in her eyes and said, "I just hope the next time you're at a party you don't make the same mistake."

Too often we hear stories like this around our neighborhood, at school, but also in Hollywood. Stars like Brittney Murphy, Heath Ledger, Casey Johnson, and DJ AM, and many others who have all died from bad choices. People like Kelly Osbourne, Nicole Richie, David Arquette, and many others chose to use their bad experiences with drugs and alcohol as a wakeup call. They all decided something needed to change so they made a conscious effort to get clean and sober otherwise they would have lost everything. You really have to be careful who you associate with because like Asia it can cost you your life.

When I was younger I assumed my mom was purposely messing up my social life because I thought she was so strict and did not let me do things that my friends could. It was only as I got older that I understood that she only made those choices and rules to protect me from hurt or making the same mistakes she did. Have you ever sat down and thought about why your parents do not want you to hang around certain people? Sometimes they can see what you don't and they are trying to protect you from getting hurt and making bad decisions. "I can't wait to get out of the house" is what I said and what I have heard other kids say growing up. It seems like parents just don't understand what you are going through and that they are just trying to ruin your life.

You must remember that your parents were your age once believe it or not. Of course times have changed but the issues that you face are still similar to what they went through it just looks different. Even though your parent(s) may get on your last nerve do you think there intention is to really hurt you? If you believe that they have bad intentions and that they are putting you in danger then you need to speak with someone. For those of you who answered no give your parents a break and let some of their information sink in a little.

Regardless of what your parents are riding you about know that every day that you wake up you have a choice. We have a lot of excuses for our behavior but at the end of the day we all have choices. Even though you may not be doing anything you could be guilty by association. Have you ever heard the saying, "Birds of a feather flock together?" For example, if you hang around people who sell drugs, steal, prostitute themselves, or are in a gang people will label you as well. I'm not saying stop being there friend but you have to create some boundaries so you do not get caught up in anything shady or suspect.

You can get shot, beat up, locked up, or raped just because you are hanging around people who are making bad decisions. If that person cared about you they would never put you or allow you into any situation that could be detrimental. Always make sure you surround yourself with people who are going somewhere in life and who make good decisions.

Some Good Choices
Going to school
Following rules
Making good decisions
Telling the truth
Admitting when you are wrong

Some Bad Choices
Using drugs
Having unprotected sex
Stealing
Lying
Manipulating

I know you get the picture so why is it so hard to make the good choices? Somehow it has become cool to make bad decisions because everyone is doing it. If you really sit back and think, "Are these people really happy?" your answer will more than likely be no. Usually, friends who are doing drugs are trying to escape from something that they do not know how or do not want to deal with. For the ones who are having sex they are looking for someone to fill a void in their life. Once you give yourself away sexually you can never get that moment back. We will talk more about this in the last chapter.

People do things for a lot of reasons and I can guarantee you that if they are doing something that can hurt themselves or you that is a person who you do not want to be involved with. Let me ask you something; if a person does not care about themselves what makes you think they care about you?

What would you do if someone told you to:

➢ Just sniff a little bit

➢ Take a sip I promise nothing will happen to you I got your back

➢ Just go to this party for me

➢ Tell my parents I am staying at your house

➢ Put this in your bag and act normal

➢ Let me put it in one time I promise you I will stop

In every one of these situations you have a choice and it is up to you to make the right one. Whatever you decide know that there are consequences some short and long term. In every situation that you face think before you act because it could cost you your life. Loving yourself is not an option or a choice it is something that you must do. If you do not love yourself how do you expect to get it back in return?

"Be careful of the company you keep"

Here are a few examples of what you could be allowing that is harmful and can affect your future:

- Allowing people to use you constantly
- Thinking it is okay for him or her to hit you because you may have said or did something wrong
- Allowing yourself to have so-called friends who are never there when you need them
- Throwing up your food
- Not exercising or eating healthy
- Having sex with any boy or girl who says they love you
- Cutting yourself
- Using drugs
- Isolating yourself
- Not asking for help when you really need it
- Continuously having babies when you cannot take care of them or yourself
- Fighting all the time
- Not going to school

If some of these things apply to you it's okay. Whatever you go through in life is meant to make you stronger. Whatever you may struggle with it is not going to change overnight so be patient and take it one day at a time.

Ask Yourself:

Where do I want to be in 5 years?

How am I going to get there?

Am I on the right path?

What do I want out of my relationships?

What do I need to change?

Who Am I?

In order to move forward in life you have to have goals, a plan, and a vision so that you can achieve your dreams and accomplish them without any distractions. When you have a plan put in place it helps guide you in the right direction so you know where you want to go and what you need to do to get there. When you know what you want in your relationships whether it is with family members or with a girlfriend/boyfriend you know what you will and will not tolerate.

People treat you a certain way because of what you allow. For example, if you are in a romantic relationship with someone and they are always putting you down and treating you like crap it is because you allow them too. If you love yourself enough you will realize you deserve better and either check that person or let them go.

"Who Am I?" is a very important question because if you don't know who you are it is going to be difficult for others to figure that out as well. You spend so much of your time trying to be what everybody else wants you to be. It's vital to figure out who you are and love yourself regardless of what others think. God made you special and unique which means there is no one else like you! Most of the time it's a good thing to be different; I don't know if this world could handle two of me. Take time out to see what is important to you and think about your future.

Yeah, you are having fun now but that same fun can cost you more than you're willing to pay?

You only have one life so make it count!

"If you don't stand for something you will fall for anything"

I PROMISE

I promise today that I will quit I just need one more hit
I really don't have a problem so I know I can beat this

Everyone's freaking out like I don't have this under control
I wish they would just get off my back this "I really care about you" crap is getting
old

I love the way I feel when I'm high I don't have a care in the world
He really thought I would always be his little girl

Even though I don't remember half of the stuff I do or who I do it with my excuse
is that I'm young
People act like they never had fun

Yeah I cuss out my parents when they find my stash or blow my high
It's my life who give a **** we're all going to die

It's my life
It's my choice
Who cares

Well I care
Yes I said I do
If you keep living this way you won't make to see the age of 22

Whose there for you when the world has turned its back
Who would have ever thought you'd be addicted to heroin, cocaine, pills, and crack

It's not too late you still have a choice
I don't want to make the decision for you because you have your own voice

I promise I won't leave you I'll be here after you receive help
I'm here
As long as you hold on to God's unchanging hand there will be nothing to fear

You're almost there please take that step
I can hear you through your tears
I can hear you crying for help

For more information about drugs go to **http://www.abovetheinfluence.com**

February
LOL

"Communication"

Jessica and her dad fought like crazy all the time. Jessica thought her dad was from a different planet and spoke some unknown language. Every time Jessica tried to talk to her dad about anything it would end up in an argument. One day when Jessica came home from school with one of her friends her dad was waiting for her at the kitchen table with an attitude. Jessica's dad called her into the kitchen to talk about what he had found in her room. She was not surprised when her dad had a blunt sitting on the table because she had been smoking weed for about a year now. Jessica dropped her books and just stared at her dad like she was confused about the whole situation. Jessica's dad saw right through her act and asked her how long she had been smoking.

Her dad asked her again how long she had been smoking marijuana and Jessica was honest and told him. Her dad was so shocked that he reached across the table and tried to grab her. Jessica's friend ran in and calmed the father down. All her father could do was ask, "Why would you do this we have talked about drugs, you know your grandma used drugs? Look what it did to her and our family, how could you?" Jessica replied, "All you do is compare me to her when I screw up so I figured why not be like her so it could be true. When you say crazy things about me that aren't true it just makes me want to go out it and do it. You always said I act like a pot head so I decided to see what an actual pot head is like." All Jessica's dad could do was sit there and cry. He finally stopped sniffling and asked Jessica why she didn't just tell him how

29

upset his words had hurt her instead of doing drugs. Jessica said, "I can't talk to because you

always think I am doing something wrong."

LOL, SMH, IDK, LMBO, WTH, etc. are just a few acronyms that are used on a daily basis using text messages, Facebook, MySpace, Twitter, etc. The way we communicate is so important because it says a lot about ourselves (education, status, our upbringing). When it comes to parents it is hard for them to keep up with technology and today's language so they can understand you. When you learn how to communicate what you feel and what you want; it makes life a whole lot easier especially when dealing with your parents.

Parents

When you hold everything inside that is where a lot of your anger comes from. When you do not deal with that anger that is where the bad choices come from. All Jessica had to do was tell her dad how she really felt instead of choosing to smoke weed to prove a point. I could have avoided so many arguments with my parents if I simply told them what was bothering me. When I did get the nerve it usually came out the wrong way because I was angry. So, if your parents make you angry let them know but in a respectful way. I don't want you to get slapped because of this book lol!

Example of communicating to your parents:
Mom: You are so lazy, you never do anything. Your sister always does her chores and her homework by the time I get home. What's your problem?

Ray: I had a long day at school and I'm just tired.

Ray: I'm sorry I haven't been pulling my share around here but when you say things like that it makes me feel even worse.

Mom: I shouldn't have yelled at you and I have had a long day too so I know how you feel. Just help me out a little more okay.

Ray: I will

Okay I know this sounded a little corny but it is just an example. What I really want you to understand is that the way you say things and your tone (the way you speak) is important. Have you heard the saying, "It's not what you say, it's how you say it". Parents and others are going to be more receptive if you approach them with less attitude. I have always had a problem with my mouth and still do. I felt like everything I had to say was important regardless if I was wrong or not. As I got older I had to learn that I am not always right and that I don't know everything (which was HARD and still is).

School

Teachers are like parents except for they have more kids to watch and attend to. If you need help ask. I remember my senior year of high school I struggled in College Algebra. I managed to come out with a D the first semester. I knew that I had to get my grade up so I got help every morning before school from my teacher. Once she knew exactly what I struggled with I was able to learn the material better and the second semester I got a B. This not only applies to schoolwork but also if you are having problems with bullies. There are too many kids out there now and days' taking their lives because of bullies at school and that does not have to be you. If the principle will not listen tell a teacher, and if that does not work keep telling people until you find someone that will listen.

Relationships

If you are in a relationship and you want it to be successful then you have to communicate. Some people are kind of slow when it comes to relationships so you need to tell them your wants and needs. Too often people assume that the other person automatically knows what they want when that is not the case. If you do not want to have sex you need to be upfront about it in the beginning so they do not expect it later on. If you just want to be friends inform the person before their feelings get hurt. When you get upset about something talk about it when you both are in a good space and not when both of you are upset.

Guys I just want to let you know in case you don't already that some girls are emotional creatures. Some girls come with a lot of hormones and require a great deal of patience at times. When girls know that you are truly listening then they know you care. That is not always the case but it is important to give that special someone your undivided attention.

So, put down your cell phone, PlayStation or x-box 360 remote and give her your undivided attention. I promise you it will save you a lot of drama. Girls you are not off the hook; know that guys are different from us so we cannot expect them to be as emotional. Take the time to understand where he is coming from as well.

Tips on How to Communicate Better:

- ❖ Wait until your parent(s) has calmed down before you talk to them
- ❖ Say it in a respectful tone
- ❖ Listen to them too
- ❖ Admit when you are wrong
- ❖ Make sure that there are no distractions and that they have your full attention

If you cannot talk to your parents go to someone you can trust so you can release your frustration and anger. Once you communicate your issues to that person they can help you come up with solutions.

"If you never tell anyone how you feel, how are they supposed to know?"

HEAR ME

I try to communicate how I feel but I think it's going through one ear and out of the other
I don't want to keep nagging you because I'm your girlfriend not your mother

You never want to spend time together you are always with your friends
I'm trying to hang in there but I just want this relationship to end

Every time I call you push forward and go on with your day
I swear I'm to my breaking point I have nothing more to say

I'm not a quitter because I tried but you wouldn't open your ears or your eyes
It's no need to prolong the inevitable we might as well say our goodbyes

I pray the next girl has patience and doesn't really talk
Because dating someone as whack as you was no walk in the park

Maybe you'll answer your phone and stop spending so much time with your friends
and say what's on your mind

All I wanted was a conversation from time to time, was that too much to ask
Well I'm moving on to my future
You are no longer in my present
because now you're my past

March
Hear Me

"You have a voice"

I know many times you feel like you don't have a voice because you are not an adult yet but you do. Some things that you do not have a say in is going to school, chores, curfew, etc. You do have a say in:

- ❖ What you want to do with your life
- ❖ How you want to be treated
- ❖ What you want people to know
- ❖ Your opinion and beliefs

I felt frustrated as a child because I had a lot to say but was always shut down by teachers because I talked too much. That problem has still not gone away but it is a good thing because now I talk about stuff that matters (most of the time). Knowing that my voice mattered was important to me because I was somebody too. Your parents cannot live your life for you because you have to decide what is best for your future. If what makes you happy is laying around all day, kicking it with friends 24/7, asking people for money constantly, smoking weed or other drugs all the time then that is your choice. If this is what your definition of happy is then maybe you need to reevaluate some things and take a hard look at your life.

Ask Yourself:

How long do you plan on doing this?

Where will this lead me?

Is there a future for me if I continue down this path?

How will this affect others around me?

Will I be financially prepared for the world?

At the end of the day you have to do what makes you happy because it is your life. I am not saying you should choose to live on the streets because your parents want you to go to college or to directly disobey your parents because you feel like it. I'm not trying to get your parents to go to jail for hurting you because of something you read in this book. So please do not tell your parents I said you can do what you want because I don't want to get slapped either.

I am saying if your parents want you to go to school for business and you want to study dance make the choice for you. You are going to be mad at yourself in the long run if you are always choosing what everybody else wants for you. You may have to sacrifice money and get your own loans but it is your decision. Imagine working a corporate job and daydreaming non-stop about designing cars, dancing, or owning your own bakery. You do have a choice but do not go into your dream blindly without any research. For example, if you want to go to a big college and know that you will not be able to afford it then you have to make some hard choices. You may have to go to a junior college first and save up or go somewhere else. You have to be realistic as well and step back and evaluate everything. I am sure your parents will take you more seriously if they feel you know what you are talking about and have a detailed plan on how you plan to achieve your dream.

You have a say in how you want to be treated. People will only treat you the way you allow them too. If you are wondering why everybody treats you like trash it is because you allow them to. If someone is not treating you the way you think they should it is up to you to change it. Sitting there griping and complaining about the situation is not going to make that person change. You need to surround yourself with people who add to your life instead of people who take from it.

People Who Add	People Who Take Away
-Encourage you	-Always negative
-Pray for you	-Always gossiping
-Forgive you	-Tearing you down
-Always there	-Complaining
-Listen	-Selfish
-Considerate	-Always involved in drama

Whoever comes to mind if they have 3 or more of the take away traits you probably need to drop them out of your life. No one is perfect but if they are not willing to change some of those bad habits you may have to drop them like one. You cannot move forward with friends like that. Remember "Misery loves company" and that "Hurt people hurt people." You will make better choices when you surround yourself with positive people who want to see you do well. Also evaluate what type of friend you are and which category you fall into. If you are a negative person you will get negativity back. If you are a positive person well you know the rest!

People only know what you tell them so be careful who you tell your business to. So, many times we confide in people who we think are our friends and then you hear from someone else something you told them in confidence. I have a couple of people that I tell everything too because I know I can trust them and then I have people in my life that I cannot tell anything personal to because everyone will know. You can tell if this person will tell your business because they are always telling someone else's. Just think if they are telling you everyone else's business what makes you think they won't tell yours (because they are your friend). Remember that the person who they are gossiping is their friend too!

It is vital that you have your own mind and think for yourself. This separates the leaders from the followers. So many times you get caught up in what everyone else is doing that you just go with the flow. Being a leader is not caring what others think about you and being confident in who you are. If you are not confident with yourself you let other people's opinions define who you are. Even if you have to stand alone at least you stick to what you believe and don't conform to other people's opinions about you.

YOUR VOICE MATTERS!!!!!!!!!!!!!!!!!!!!!!!!!!!!!!!!!!

Katy dreaded going to her math class every day because Mr. Bruno made every day a living hell. He embarrassed students just because he could and all of the kids knew that teachers could not get fired once they had tenure. She felt like she had no power and it was really getting to her. On this one particular day Mr. Bruno asked Katy to come to the front of the class. He gave her a quiz she had took last week and told her to read the score on the front out loud. It was an F and she soon realized that he was trying to embarrass her. In front of the class Mr. Bruno told the students, "This is what happens when you don't study and whenever anyone gets an F I will make them stand in front of the class." Katy was so mad that she ran out of the classroom and ran straight to the office. She told the principal what happened and that she wanted to call her parents. The principal asked if she had any proof of this and of course she didn't. "Why would I lie about this," Katy replied. The principal looked at her sincerely and said, "I am not saying that you are a liar but I hire all of the teachers and I have never heard a complaint from anyone else."

Katy felt so small and helpless. If her own principal didn't believe her how was she going to convince her parents? She came up with a plan because you could always count on Mr. Bruno to embarrass someone for his enjoyment. The next day Katy brought a recorder to class and recorded Mr. Bruno tearing down another student in front of the class. Katy took her story to a news station who was shocked by this teacher. The story made it to the 5 o'clock news that day and an immediate investigation was done at the school. Reporters asked the principal if anyone has every complained and Katy looked from a distance and smiled. Katy realized at that very moment that her voice mattered and that she stood up for herself and the entire school.

<u>VOICE</u>

Why won't anybody listen I'm practically screaming at the top of my lungs

I bet I would turn heads if I shot this gun

What I have to say is important and I want you to listen
If anyone ignores me someone is going to come up missing

Okay, now that I have your attention forget about what I just said
I knew that would make you turn my way

It's not surprising that I have to say crazy things to get you to listen
to what I have to say

I have decided that I'm going to run for president or maybe settle for vice
I know what you're thinking
that may not be very wise

Yeah my grades suck and I'm not on any committees
But I have a long time to rebuild my rep and I'm starting with this city

The first thing I'm going to change is this crappy school lunch and less time
in class
Allow all students to roam the halls whenever they want without a hall pass

Make parents give their kids a large allowance at least twice a month
And make it mandatory to have free deodorant in gym class because that's
just too much funk

Extend summer vacation because I need more time to rest
And get into any college without taking the ACT or SAT test

I know it sounds outrageous but look at all the stuff nobody thought would
pass
and when it does everybody will kissing my

Now that you know my plans you now have a choice
You can let me have a later curfew, date whoever I want, and drive your car
Or in about 25 years I will be this countries voice

Spring

April
Me, Me, Me

"Victim"

"This always happens to me."

"Nothing good ever happens."

"After what I have been through can you blame me?"

"I always mess up so it doesn't even matter."

"Every time I try people always try to mess with me."

If you find yourself or anyone that you know continually using phrases similar to the ones above something is not right. When someone continually blames things on the world or themselves they are suffering from what we like to call "Victim Mentality". This is something that you do not want to catch because it is hard to get rid of. Always blaming stuff on yourself or others handicaps you because you are never accountable for what you do. Sometimes people blame things on themselves because it is easier even if it is not their fault or they did do something wrong but is never their fault.

People who have a victim mentality receive a lot of attention and validation; they do not have to take many risks, and do not have as many responsibilities as others. By getting attention from others this way it tires people out because they always have to comfort that person and help them with every situation. Imagine if you had a friend who always cried about how horrible their family life was, how they always got into with their boyfriend/girlfriend, the list goes on and it is never their fault. A person suffering from victim mentality is scared to fail or be rejected which is part of life. You are not going to get every job, win every event, get accepted to every college, and that is okay. When I first started applying to colleges I wanted to go to Spelman or Hampton University and I did not apply because I was scared that I wouldn't get in. Looking back I wish I would have tried anyway because to this day I will never know what the outcome could have been.

Denying yourself opportunities because of fear is detrimental because you never allow yourself to take chances. If you fail, dust your feet off, and try again. When I worked in residential facilities it was really painful to watch young men and women suffer because of their poor choices or from their parents. Even though my heart cried for them I wanted to challenge them to be better and to do better. I did not want them to have a pity party because of poor decisions. Regardless of what has happened to you or what you are going through right now it is up to you to be better because life is what you make it.

No one makes you:
- Do drugs
- Skip school
- Drink and drive
- Have sex with whomever
- Become physically, mentally, or emotionally abusive
- Cut yourself
- Starve yourself or eat too much

You have to be responsible for YOU and make the choice to be better, to be different, and to be stronger. Coming from a destructive family does not help and can hinder you from being the best you can be but it is up to you to make that change. It's your choice whether you let bad circumstances defeat you or whether you use it to push you towards greatness. My husband grew up with 5 siblings and his mother on the Southside of Chicago. He was surrounded by gangs, witnessed drive-by, watched friends and people around the neighborhood become addicted to drugs, got robbed, and watched other types of violence. Growing up in that type of environment leaves you with only two paths the right one or the wrong one. He still made the choice to do the right thing despite all the madness around him. Luckily for him his mother and brothers did not allow him to go the negative route so going down the wrong path was never an option. Unfortunately other people around him were not as lucky and did not make it out of the hood. Despite his surroundings and all the chaos that he saw he went on to college and majored in engineering and because of his choices he is reaping the benefits.

Quiz

*Circle **yes** if you agree with the statement or circle **no** if you disagree:*

When I know I did something wrong I usually blame it on someone else.	Y or N
I am accountable for my actions.	Y or N
The world is always against me.	Y or N
Bad things always happen to me.	Y or N
I always mess up and it's my fault.	Y or N
I know some things you cannot control.	Y or N
Good things happen to me.	Y or N
I have trouble making decisions.	Y or N
I usually follow what others do.	Y or N
I make excuses when I get caught.	Y or N

If you answered yes to 4 or more you may be struggling with victim mentality.

10 Ways to get rid of Victim Mentality

1. When you know better you do better. So now that you know better start making an effort to change.

2. Admit when you are wrong. As long as you dwell on a situation you are going to continue to feel sorry for yourself.

3. You are always going to experience unpleasant things and everything that we go through in life is a test. Take every trial as a lesson learned. Learn something from the situation so that the next time it comes up you know how to deal with it.

4. You are not the only one going through something. Remember someone always has it worse than you.

5. Do not dwell on the past because it is just that the past. If someone hurt you forgiveness needs to be the next step so you can move on. Life is too short to be unhappy and you need to enjoy it while you can because tomorrow is promised to no one.

6. Don't be so hard on yourself. If you mess up "SO WHAT" try again and again. You are always going to make mistakes. It is what you do after those mistakes that matters the most.

7. Please do not use other people as an excuse as to why you fail. You are giving that person power over your life and you don't even know it.

8. Have someone hold you accountable. It helps to have people remind you of when you are acting like a victim.

9. Remind yourself that YOU are responsible for your happiness

10. Be accountable for your actions because you owe it to yourself.

When a person has a victim mentality it is all about them because only their feelings, wants, and needs matter. When a person asks you "What's in it for me?" that is not a good sign because it is good thing to do things for others without expecting anything in return. I have seen some people who always expect a gift or to be compensated for something that should have been a gift or a blessing to someone. When it is all about you the people around you suffer. For instance, your teacher assigns a group project and a person in the group tries to take all of the credit when everyone put in the same amount of time and effort. Another example would be a group of friends that are trying to do something special for someone but one person makes the situation all about them and their needs. People who fall into this category do not care about other people because they only care about themselves. People who are selfish will lose friends easily and will realize sooner or later that life does not revolve around them. Once you start caring about the needs of others you will start to see that there is more to life than YOU. Imagine what the world would look like if everybody thought of other people.

How do you know if you are selfish?
1. Only look out for #1 (yourself)
2. Will do anything to get ahead even if that means hurting others
3. You always want more even though you have enough
4. Inconsiderate of other people's feelings
5. You never listen to anybody but you always want to explain yourself
6. Do not care who you hurt

Practice Being Thankful

- Thank God every day for what and who you have
- Check your attitude
- Show by your actions how grateful you are
- Give back to others

What are you grateful for?

_____

_____

_____

_____

At Christmas, on birthdays, and at the beginning of school you expect new things but what happens when you don't get them? Some people do not get anything on these special occasions so it is important that you are grateful for what you have and whatever you receive. Remember someone always has it worse off than you.

When you are grateful for the little things it makes you appreciate everything you receive especially when it is unexpected. For example, in college I drove an 89' Toyota Camry with rust stains and a broken window that had a trash bag on it. I know what you're thinking but I still thought I was cute lol. I loved my car because I could go wherever I wanted and I didn't have to ask anybody for a ride. I took care of it and appreciated it because it was mine. Years later I was blessed with the car of my dreams a Dodge Charger. I was so grateful for that Camry that when I got a new car it made me appreciate it that much more!

****Activity****

Pick 10 people and write them a letter thanking them for something they did for you.

CONSUMED

As the flames begin to increase so does my anger

The smoke is uncontrollable but I am familiar to the unsafe conditions

I always find a way out

After this terrible tragedy there is so much damage the estimate cannot even be configured

Guess that means I will have to start all over again

Starting over means from the ground up

So I will have to get a new foundation (renewed faith)
New windows (renewed eyes)
New door (renewed spirit)

The house that burned down was me
When the flames enveloped me that was jealousy, hurt, pain, and anger that took over my being

But faith in God and his unconditional love has given my life a brand new meaning

The smoke was negativity that tried to consume my mind with negative thoughts such as:
She will never love you
It was your fault
You will never change
Sex is the only thing that will make him stay
And you were never planned for God's pleasure from the beginning you were a mistake

My negative thoughts wanted me to have a victim mentality and believe it only happened to me

I have to stop depending on myself and others for advice that only God can give
And the only person's life I should be modeling is Jesus' because he taught us how to live

God said that he will never leave me nor forsake me but how could this be true when he allowed me to go through such horrible things and experience things a child should never have to go through or see

As I have grown I have realized that everyone in the bible was tested and those very tests made them into the person God wanted them to be

For without tests testimonies would not exist and everyone would be discouraged
Well this is my testimony and I want you to be encouraged

I am a living witness of what God can do
and for every bad situation that I have experienced in my life Kerra has come through

<u>*May*</u>
It's Not My Fault

"Accountability"

If the teacher would have listened to me she would have known that I was upset.

He knew that I did not want to have sex with him so I didn't feel like I had to say something.

Maybe if you guys practiced more this team wouldn't suck.

If you did not work so much I wouldn't be in so much trouble.

If my daddy had not left I would not have this problem.

I just wanted her to love me and she couldn't even do that.

Growing up I never wanted to be accountable (responsible for my actions) for anything I did; whether it was getting caught having sex, getting a bad grade, or breaking curfew. I had a reason for everything and it was never my fault. It's easier to blame somebody or a situation for your mistakes because you never have to be accountable. People have more respect for you when you can admit that you're wrong, when you can apologize, and when you can move forward.

<u>How can you be more accountable:</u>

- Admit when you are wrong

- Apologize

- Ask for forgiveness when needed

- Own your feelings

- Be honest

Take a minute and write down some things you haven't been accountable for.

1.

2.

3.

4.

What can you do to change it?

_____

_____

_____

_____

_____

_____

Greg was going to high school this year and only had one thing on his mind and that was playing on the high school basketball team. At 14 he was already 6"1" and had made a name for himself on the courts around his neighborhood. When he went out for tryouts he not only impressed his future teammates but also all the coaches. When the coaches posted who was going to be on Junior Varsity and Varsity Greg knew where his name was. He was so excited to be on Varsity but didn't know that the girls would be all over him. He made every practice and worked on his game 24/7. His coach saw his commitment and when the season started he decided to let him become a starter. The ladies started to notice Greg and Greg started to notice the ladies. His parents had always warned him to focus on school and playing basketball; everything else was forbidden like dating and hanging out with his friends. He was not allowed to date or go to parties because of his strict parents but of course he always found a way around that. Greg was always one of the best players at his games. He scored on average 20 points and averaged at least 11 rebounds.

After one of his games he noticed a girl named Stacey checking him out. Now Stacey was one of the prettiest girls in the school who could have any guy she wanted. Stacey was tall too with almond skin, gray eyes, had a nice cropped hair cut, and a body to die for. The fact that she was checking Greg out made him smile and think he had a chance one day. Well that day finally came after a game and Stacey approached him and asked if he wanted to grab something to eat and of course he said yes. After he got cleaned up he met Stacey outside and went to grab some hamburgers and fries at a local restaurant.

After they ate dinner Stacey invited Greg to her house and when they got there she invited him up to her room to "talk". Without hesitation he walked up to her room not knowing that it would change his life forever. Greg did not know that her parents were gone and were not coming back until the next morning. While sitting on her bed they started to make out and when both of their clothes came off Greg asked if she had a condom and she said, "I'm on the pill". He didn't know much about sex but knew that if she was on something then she couldn't possibly get pregnant and she looked too good to have an STD. Greg was fine with that answer and decided to have sex with her anyway. After they were finished Greg felt like the big man on campus and wanted the world to know that he was in love. After that night Greg and Stacey were inseparable and started having sex all the time.

After every game Stacey and Greg would hang out but lately Greg had been noticing that Stacey was acting weird. He wanted to know what was up and asked her if everything was cool. Stacey immediately started crying and told him she missed her period. Greg did not know what to say but all he could think about was his future and losing out on his big basketball career. Greg got so upset at the thought of losing his basketball career because of this baby news that he flipped out and accused her of purposely getting pregnant. Stacey was hurt and told him she was on the pill but forgot a couple of times. This was not the first time that she forgot and nothing ever happened so she did not think it was a big deal. Greg told her he would help get rid of her problem but would need some time. Stacey looked up confused and asked, "What are you talking about I'm not getting an abortion." Greg replied, "Well if you don't get one I'm not helping you and who knows if I'm the father anyway. You gave it up so easily the first time we met. How do I know I am the only one?" Stacey got up and walked away feeling like trash and realized that she was on her own. Both of their worlds were shattered and nothing could turn back the hands of time to change the present.

What should Greg have done to be more accountable?

_____

_____

_____

_____

_____

What should Stacey have done to be more accountable?

_____

_____

_____

_____

_____

How will their lives change?

_____

_____

_____

_____

_____

A show like *16 and Pregnant* is a great example of young teens not being accountable and paying for it by going through unnecessary pain and heartache. Before you blame or accuse someone of wrong doing always check yourself first. At times we forget to look at ourselves to see if we could have done everything in our power in certain situations.

You are always going to go through something in life so there is no use in having a pity party. You can never prepare yourself for the storms in life but you can make sure that you have healthy ways of dealing with them. You can become really stressed out when you are dealing with a lot of drama so it is important that you learn how to deal with it. When I get stressed I usually turn to pizza and ice cream but over the years I realized my stomach and my thighs were beginning to spread. So, I had to find healthier ways to deal with my issues. People cope with stress in different ways so it is important that you find the right coping skill(s) such as: writing, reading, exercising, talking to someone, drawing, laughing, listening to music, or anything that makes you happy (no drugs or alcohol)! Even though drugs and alcohol may make you happy the feeling that you get from them only last temporarily. Finding a healthy coping mechanism last a lot longer and can help you make better choices.

What are some issues that you are dealing with? How are you dealing with them?

_____

_____

_____

_____

Write down some ways that you can cope?

_____

_____

_____

_____

<u>SORRY</u>

I know time heals all wounds I just hope yours heal without scars
I didn't know the rumors weren't true I didn't think it would go that far

You can't blame just me everyone had something to say
You need to stop being so sensitive and deal with it

You didn't deny anything so I took everything with a grain of salt
I know I'm your best friend but you have to take responsibility it wasn't my fault

I told you not to go to his house but you thought it would make you cool
I didn't want to say I told you so but you made yourself look like a fool

With every choice you make you have to know that there are consequences
whether they are good or bad

Next time you will listen

June
Move On

"Living in the Past"

Alley and her brother Carlos had a pretty decent life with their mother and father until things went downhill. As a family they always did everything together but things started to change and their parents starting arguing all the time. It got so bad that the neighbors had to call the police several times because they thought their parents were going to kill one another. Their parents realized how much their arguing affected the kids so they decided to get a divorce. At this time Alley was 6 and Carols was 5 when everything was final. Their mother had full custody and they got to see their father on the weekends. Everything was working out fine until their father started dating some woman. He started spending all of his time with her and less time with them. Since their father was never there they had to spend a lot of time at their grandma's house but they didn't mind because they had fun with their uncles and cousins. Their father always made it a point to be there when it was convenient for him.

Alley was 8 years old when her father got married to his new wife. Her father did not waste any time having three more kids with his new wife which meant less time with Alley and Carlos. They started to resent him for not being there and when he forgot Alley's birthday that resentment turned to hate. She wanted nothing to do with him but Carlos still hoped that his dad would change and go back to the old days of being in their lives. Alley always reminded Carlos of what a horrible father they had and how much he didn't care about them. As the years went by

Alley and Carlos became comfortable with their father's absence and realized that when he did see or talk to them it was nothing to get excited about.

Out of the blue their mother called them and told Alley and Carlos to come home early because she had to talk to them about something important. She explained to them that their dad was having problems with his wife and that they were getting a divorce. They both were unaffected by the news and didn't care but were curious as to why their mom thought it was important. Their mom told them that their father would be moving back in with them until he could get on his feet. Alley was numb and did not know how to react to this news; but deep down she felt like he got what he deserved and didn't feel bad for him. All Carlos could do was cry because he had mixed emotions. He hated him for not being there but was glad that he would be a part of his life again. Alley's dad tried to reach out to her every chance he got but Alley was not having it. She remembered him never been there for her or Carlos and reminded him of that every chance she got. In her eyes it was too late for him to try and be a father now and she didn't need him.

When you live in the past it takes away from your present. How can you move one when you are constantly worried, upset, or fearful about what "so and so" did to you, what you did not have, and so on? I was molested by my stepfather and when he got arrested I was known as the girl who had sex with her father. I could have tried to fight everybody and be upset all of the time but what would that accomplish. A lot of people who have gone through some form of abuse did not allow the abuse to hold them back from being who they were created to be. When I look back at that traumatic time I get sad sometimes but it quickly turns into a smile because I know everything that I have been through in life has made me a stronger person.

I had a lot of issues but with God and counseling I managed to get through that horrible ordeal. You need to talk to someone about what has happened to you especially if it is hindering you from being productive or moving on with your life. When you have traumatic experiences it is hard to think positive especially about the future. Imagine what life would be like if everyone was afraid to move on. For example, your parents wouldn't let you do anything or go anywhere because of their fears.

What can hold you back?

- Traumatic experiences

- Doubt

- Fear

- Yourself

It's okay to get angry but when you do not deal with it; then it becomes a problem. When it becomes a problem the people around you disappear because they do not want to deal with that.

When you are hurting and shutting everyone out it will become a lonely world but it doesn't have to be. Life sucks at times but it does get better. My abuse is a thing of the past; it does not run my life anymore I DO. I made the decision to deal with it so that I could have meaningful relationships and feel better about myself.

You hear stories about people who haven't spoken in years because of something that happened in high school, last Christmas, last summer, last night, etc. When it is all said and done life is too short to hold grudges or be upset. People waste a lot of time and energy being mad at someone for what they did to them a long time ago. One thing that you need to realize is that people change. I am not the same girl I was in high school but some people still hold a grudge for something I did or said when I was just 17. It seems silly but not to those people holding the grudge. They cannot move forward because they are living in the past. Ten years has passed and to this day I do not know why these people are mad at me and they don't either. This does not only happen with friends but with family members as well.

At the end of the day if you have issues with someone try to talk to them and try to forgive them. Sometimes people will not know that they have hurt you unless you tell them. You have to forgive them so you can move on or you will be stuck in the past too. Another tip would be to remember that everybody deserves a second chance. If you were in their position wouldn't you want a second chance? We can be here today but gone tomorrow. Remember that traumatic experiences, fear, doubt, and "yourself" are some of the things that that hold you back instead of propelling you forward. Don't live in the past, live in the present, and look forward to your future.

Even though things have been tough know that God has something better planned for you. Whatever you may be going through it is only temporary (only for a little while). It is okay to be mad or angry because someone hurt you but not for too long. If you are angry all the time how does that affect the other person? You are the one walking around angry wasting all of that energy trying to prove a point. If you can't find it in your heart to forgive that person right away take some time. You can forgive them later and still not have a relationship with that person. As long as you do your part that is all that matters.

What are some of the things holding back from being happy in the present?

_____

_____

_____

_____

What do you need to do to move forward?

_____

_____

_____

_____

<u>7 Things to Remember:</u>

1. Forgive others and yourself

2. Trust that God always has something better

3. Your situation is temporary

4. Communicate with others

5. Don't dwell on the past, it only hinders the present

6. Focus on your future

7. Everyone deserves a second chance, don't YOU

How do you feel when people disappoint you? Rate how you feel when the following situations happen (0 = Don't Care, 1 = Care, and 2 = Extremely Upset). Circle the number that would match how you feel.

1. When your girlfriend/boyfriend cheats on you   (0, 1, 2)

2. Your parent's don't keep their word   (0, 1, 2)

3. Your friends are being two-faced   (0, 1, 2)

4. People call you ugly   (0, 1, 2)

5. When people write stupid stuff on your Facebook page   (0, 1, 2)

6. When people are late   (0, 1, 2)

7. Receive a bad grade even though you know you studied   (0, 1, 2)

8. People lie   (0, 1, 2)

9. Someone wants to fight you for no reason   (0, 1, 2)

10. Feel like no one's in your corner   (0, 1, 2)

Total points: _____

If you received a 16 or higher:

You really have to work on letting stuff roll off your back because someone is always going to have something to say about you whether it is good or bad. It is important to have a good support system that encourages you and says positive things about you and to you. Regardless of what people say or do you have to be in control of your emotions and choose how you want to react.

If you received 10 to 15:

Realize it is not what people say but it is what you answer to that matters. If you let every little thing bother you I promise you that you will become a miserable person. You have to pick and choose your battles carefully because you will not win all of them.

If you received a 9 or less:

You are choosing to let some stuff go instead of being worried about every little thing. Continue to work on yourself and your emotions. Think before you speak and act because there are always consequences (good or bad).

When You Get Angry

Admit when you're angry

- If you are upset let someone know so you can vent to get some of your anger out.

Figure out what made you so mad

- Try and find out what made you so mad and why. For example, your friend said something that really hurt your feelings:
  - Did they try to do it on purpose?
  - Do you think they are the type of person to do something like that?
  - Is there anything else on your mind that you could be mad about?

Talk with the person who made you angry

- When you have calmed down and you are in a good place talk to the person who made you mad. Explain to them how they made you feel and also take the time to listen to where they are coming from too.

Try to forgive them and move on

- Life is too short to be angry about things that do not really matter. Try to forgive that person and move forward. I know some situations are harder than others so go with your heart. When you hang on to bad feelings it's going to eat at you because of all the energy that is wasted. The other person is not worried about the situation which is making you look silly.

What are some of the ways that you deal with anger?

_____

_____

_____

_____

Are you still angry at something someone did to you in the past? Is it possible for you to forgive them?

_____

_____

_____

_____

In today's society forgiveness seems like the hardest thing to do. Why is that? I used to hold grudges until one day it hit me that people have forgiven me when I messed up so what makes me so special that I can't forgive. People will always make mistakes because they are human and you have to remember that.

Now it's true that some things may take time to forgive and that's okay. Do it on your own time so you know it's sincere. Just because you forgive somebody that doesn't mean you forget or that you have to be best friends. Sometimes it's best to move on and still be friendly. Once you forgive someone try your best to let it go and try not to bring it up again. If you keep bringing the situation up it means you truly have not forgiven that person. These are questions you should ask yourself every once in a while.

Why should you forgive?

_____

_____

_____

_____

Is there something that you think is unforgiveable? Why?

_____

_____

_____

_____

Do you want to be forgiven for something?

_____

_____

_____

_____

CHOOSE

Sometimes I don't understand and I am often confused
It's hard to stop doing what you have always been use to

It's easy for me to make excuses because I can blame it all on my past
I enjoy my pity parties even though they do not last

Sometimes it is hard to get up and face the fact that this is your life

It is hard to realize your potential when the sky seems so high
It is easy to procrastinate and just watch life pass you by

Why try when you know you're going to fail
Who thinks about heaven when on earth it feels like hell

What's the point of praying when unanswered ones are still on his list
Why keep my eye on the target when everyone knows I'll miss

Why even live life if it doesn't get any better
The God I serve says live life abundantly
You can do this
we will get through this together

He does all the hard work just so you don't have to
It sounds simple because it is
just pray and watch God make it do what it do

Just try him and see if the world doesn't look a little brighter
Not only will you feel like a winner you will be considered a fighter

Because you stayed in the race you kept your eye on the prize
When you have God in your life you appreciate every moment
You appreciate being alive

Summer

July
I Can't

"You Can"

I can't play basketball, but I can serve a volleyball like there's no tomorrow

I can't put in my own weave, but I can braid

I can't afford those clothes, but I can put together a nice outfit

You get it! For every **CAN'T** there is a **CAN**. Volleyball is my favorite sport in the world and even though I can't play in the Olympics I can still play on local teams. There are always going to be some limitations but don't let that stop you from fulfilling your purpose or dreams in life. Everyone has a story but you have the pen and the power to change some chapters in your life. Starting today I want you to pick up your pen and start focusing on what you can do instead of what you can't and see how far you go. Your attitude affects others either in a positive or negative way. Whatever situations you face your attitude will determine how you deal with the situation and how you come out of it.

I have had three surgeries in the last three years and the last one I almost lost my life. I stopped breathing during the surgery and woke up on a breathing machine. When I came to I found out that part of my intestines had been removed and a couple of days later they found an abscess as well. I was in the hospital for two and half weeks and was in a lot of pain. I am very independent so the worse part for me was having to depend on other people for stuff I needed done. I am still recovering but in order to get better it was brought to my attention that my attitude had to change. If I was in a negative mood and complained all the time I would stay miserable. Once I realized okay this is my life right now, it sucks, but I'm grateful to be out of the hospital and to have my family and friends. I have to make the best out of this and enjoy my life because I only have one. The only person that can stop you from being your best is YOU. Saying "I Can't" limits your abilities and stops you from trying. Instead of saying the things you can't do start saying the things you can. Being positive in hard situations makes them easier to deal with.

If you have a negative attitude what will be a possible outcome for each situation? What are some positive ways to handle these?

- Find out you have cancer

- Find out you are pregnant

- Discover you may not graduate with your class

- Get diagnosed with an STD

- Your mom or dad lose their job

- Have to transfer to a new school your senior year

***Remember it could always be worse*

Have you ever been around somebody who always has a negative attitude? They are always complaining and seeing the worst in everything. Those are the people you do not want to be around because it may rub off on you. When certain situations arise in your life your attitude will show you who you are.

How is your attitude?

_____

_____

_____

_____

What needs to be changed?

_____

_____

_____

_____

What do you stress about?

_____

_____

_____

_____

What can you do to lessen the stress or worry?

_____

_____

_____

_____

When you stress about things you take the focus off of the important things. "You cannot worry about what you cannot control." I know you have a lot to worry about like:

- School
- Friends
- Boys/Girls
- Peer Pressure
- Bullies
- Keeping up with the trends
- Parents

So, where does worrying or stressing about the situation get you? Only worry about what you can handle and take everything else one day at a time. If you stress too much it can take a toll on your body: make you lose or gain weight, become ill, become depressed, or lose your hair. When it becomes too much pray about it and give it to God. When we learn to let go and let God it lightens our load so we can deal with other things. It is important to know that you cannot handle everything and that it is okay to ask for help. Some see asking for help as a sign of weakness but it takes heart to admit when you need some help.

Tatiana was raised in a family full of drug addicts, drug dealers, alcoholics, the list goes on. Being around people like this was normal for her and she didn't know anything else. Tatiana always believed that from birth she was destined to be a failure. Her father had been in and out of jail and never really wanted to be a part of her life. Tatiana's mother Rochelle was addicted to Heroin and alcohol. Tatiana pretty much took care of herself and her 2 younger brothers and 3 sisters. She never knew what it was like to be a kid because she had to grow up so fast. Now that Tatiana is 14 she feels like she is 30 because she has had the responsibilities of a grown woman. She has raised kids, had to cook, clean, and pay all of the bills that her mother neglected. Tatiana kept up her appearance and took good care of herself. Tatiana was average height for her age, long brown hair, long legs, and had smooth dark chocolate skin. She got made fun of because of her skin color but did not care because she knew she was beautiful. One thing her mother did instill in her was confidence for who she was. Her mother always told her how beautiful she was. She did not have the best of clothes but took care of what she had. Her mom would stay out days at a time and when she would come home she would act as if nothing had happened.

When it came time to go to school Tatiana thought it was a waste of time. Where she was from nobody thought school helped and that it was only for smart people. She had been diagnosed with ADHD and was placed in special education. She figured why try if she knew she was going to fail. One day when Tatiana was walking home from the corner store to get dinner for the night she saw the police outside of her house. She knew something wasn't right but she tried to play it cool. As she walked up to their roach infested apartment she saw her mother laid out on the floor. She knew her mother was dead and immediately started to freak out because who would take her and her siblings. She had heard horrible stories about foster care and knew she did not want to be separated. Tatiana knew her mom would eventually die and had already shed her tears. As the ambulance left so did her future; she knew at that moment that her life would take her on a journey that she would never forget. Social Services came and picked up Tatiana and her little brothers and sisters. Tatiana pleaded with the case worker to keep them together but the lady said that there were too many of them to put in one home. Tatiana slowly got up from the chair and turned to her brothers and sisters and started to cry. The next day Tatiana was sent to live with a foster mom named Sara Bruce. Ms. Bruce had 3 other foster kids living with her ages 10 (Layla), 12 (Tiffany), and 16 (Shay). Tatiana was scared but did not let it show because she did not want the girls to think that she was a punk. She did not talk to anyone and stayed to herself. Tatiana thought about her brothers and sisters every day and that is the only thing that kept her going.

One day when she was sitting in her room minding her own business Ms. Bruce called her to come downstairs. This was not unusual but the tone in her voice let her know that something was up. As she walked down the stairs Ms. Bruce and the 3 other girls were looking at her like she was the scum of the earth. "Tatiana when I let kids come into my home I expect them to be honest and follow my rules." Tatiana never even left her room so she was confused as to where this conversation was going. "The girls told me that you stole $60 from my purse and I want it back. Nothing is going to happen to you I just want the money back." Tatiana looked at the oldest Shay and saw that she was smiling. All she could do was ball her fist up and swing towards her direction. Once she started hitting Shay nobody could get her off. She finally snapped out of it and Ms. Bruce told her that she would have to find somewhere else to stay. "I have never stolen anything in my life and I would never steal from you," said Tatiana. "These girls would not lie and I want you out of here," Ms. Bruce yelled. While Shay was picking her mouth up from the floor she told Ms. Bruce, "I told you she was crazy you can't believe anything she says." Tatiana was in and out of foster homes for years and never graduated high school. After she lost contact with her siblings she felt she had nothing else to live for until she ran into Alecia. Alecia was short, had brown skin, big eyes, short blonde hair, and a beautiful smile. Something about her made you feel at peace but she couldn't put her finger on it. Alecia worked at a local community center and would see Tatiana around the way sometimes. As fate would have it Tatiana walked in one day and Alecia asked to talk to her.

Alecia: "I see you walk by here every day but you never come in."

Tatiana: "I figured today I would try something different."

Alecia: "Where are you from?"

Tatiana: "The Southside I live on 79th and exchange."

Alecia: "You're a long way from home"

Tatiana: "I have never had a home"

Alecia: "Why don't you stay around for a while and let me introduce you to some of the young people here"

Tatiana: "Naw, I'm good I don't get along with people that well"

She introduced Tatiana to a couple of kids who seemed friendly but Tatiana knew better so she kept her guard up. Alecia invited her to church that night but Tatiana said no. "I'm really not into God he hasn't done nothing for me and besides the whole Jesus freak thing creeps me out." Alecia laughed and said, "I know what you mean but it's not that type of group. We don't pretend to be holier than thou because we know we are human. We just try to live every day with gratitude and make the best of life because you only have one. Just give it a try and come with me to youth group tonight. "I'm cool maybe some other time," Alecia mumbled as she walked *away. It was something different about those kids that made Tatiana come back the next day. They weren't like the pastors she had seen on television or the other men and women from the previous churches she attended. They didn't force God on her and she liked that.*

When she walked in one of the recreational rooms they were praying and someone mentioned her name. No one ever prayed for her and she did not know how to react. She had been standing there for so long that when she looked up everybody was staring at her. They knew that she did not want God in her life but were determined to show her that she needed him more than anything. One of the group members told her, "Tatiana God is who he is to you and that's it. You love him in your own way and develop your own personal relationship. We are not perfect and we don't pretend to be. We are just grateful for what God has done in our lives and want to share that with others." Tatiana sat through their discussion session and was amazed at how they talked to each other, how they treated each other, how many things they did for the community, and how they treated everybody with love. She had never had that and wanted it. She asked what she could do to join and made it her mission to never look back.

NO HOPE

No one cares about me so why should I care about myself

The streets are set up to trap you

It's just me out here and nobody else

These people think they can give me the world but my world is gone

There is nothing to live for

I wish I could just die or find a place that I could call home

It is hard out here when you have to make it on your own

See it is hard out here for me and that is what nobody understands

I'm reaching out for my soul to be rescued but the only cure people tell me I need
is a man

I tried that route and didn't get to far

See they were just looking for something else

I wanted to offer somebody more than just myself

I am tired of this life I am tired of this pain

I hope one day I can see the sunshine

Even through the rain

August
No One Understands

"Putting Yourself in Other People's Shoes"

You never know what anyone is going through until you put yourself in their shoes. At school you may wonder about the person who

> - Always cuts class
> - Is always high
> - Sleeps around
> - Fights any and everyone

The person who always acts out in class may need some attention because he or she is not getting any at home, may love being the center of attention, or simply just wants to be cool. The kid who stays high may not want to deal with reality, is hurting, or has a horrible addiction that needs to be addressed. The boy or girl who sleeps around with people may be looking for someone to love them, have low self-esteem, or wants to be accepted by the opposite sex. The one thing that they all have in common is that they all want attention. Some people do not know how to go about getting attention the right way. If you are a person who dislikes these types of behaviors try to be understanding before you judge.

Do you know how powerful words are? With social networks like MySpace, Facebook, & Twitter people have used them to support and build people up but also to torment and tease people. People post nude pictures no one is supposed to see or write nasty things on other people's wall. Words can lead people to commit suicide or harm themselves in other ways like cutting, throwing up their food, bullying other people, etc. Phoebe Prince was a 15 year old girl who was a victim of cyber-bullying from the girls at her school who had a problem with who she was dating. Two days before a big dance she hung herself in her room. Jaheem Herrea and Carl Joesph both 11 year olds were being called gay every day and getting bullied in school and committed suicide as well.

Instead of criticizing someone for their differences or their actions try helping them instead and watch their reaction. If you are constantly calling someone stupid or fat how is that going to make them lose weight or get any smarter? It is best to think before you speak because you never know how your words will affect someone else.

Encourage

- If you need help with something let me know
- I have some great clothes at home that I don't wear you can have them
- I know you feel uncomfortable with your weight we can work out together
- People are saying you sleep around a lot so I would be careful
- You're different and that's cool

Discourage

- You're stupid
- Do you use a mirror at home
- Your fat
- You need to eat you are so skinny
- You're a hoe
- You're gay

*****Activity*****

Material: paper and pens
Group of people: 5-10

Directions: Fold the paper into three sections. On the outside of the paper write your name. Pass the paper around and on the inside write something nice about the other person and keep passing until you receive yours.

After you're done:

How does it feel when people say nice things about you?

_____

_____

_____

_____

How does it feel to say nice things about others?

_____

_____

_____

_____

"Remember is not what you say but how you say it"

88

Gossiping leads to a lot of fights and misunderstandings because it is usually made up or the facts are all wrong. Have you ever played the telephone game? Well prepare yourself to see what gossiping looks like. The saying "sticks and stones my break my bones but words will never hurt me" may work for some but words really do hurt. Once they leave your mouth you cannot take them back. If you want people to encourage you and to say good things about you then you have to do it as well. People may still have negative things to say but that's their problem. Obviously they are dealing with issues within themselves that you cannot fix. The only person who can change them is themselves. Be an example to others and I promise you good things will come back to you!

*****Activity*****

Get in a group of 7-10 people. Pick one person to think of a long sentence. Stand in a circle and tell the person you picked to whisper their sentence to the person beside them and pass it on. You cannot repeat yourself to the other person. When the last person hears it they have to say it out loud. Once you've done it a couple of times share amongst each other how gossip has affected you or someone you know.

DIFFERENT

You think God makes mistakes
Well I do

He put me in the wrong body and people say I'm confused

I can't help who I'm attracted to
I have felt this way since I can remember

People look at me like this is an act
Trust me this is not rehearsed

I just want to prove I am human
I am just like everybody else

Can't blame me for being honest with myself

Why can't people understand that this is who I am
It shouldn't matter if I prefer a woman or a man

Were all God's children right
so why is it that when you talk about me it is never out of love
Why is everybody so focused on my sexuality
What happened to we are not supposed to judge

All I am asking for is a little support, love, and acceptance

Stop looking on the outside
Look at my heart and then give me a chance to show you

ME

September
Outcast

"It's OK to be Different"

I have always been different and never really fit in with the "popular crowd" and my mom told me that God sets us apart because we are special. I know it sounds like something you hear in Sunday school but when I look at my life today it rings true. Being different gives you options because you are not stuck in everyone's mold of what you should be. I have tried to be that a girl who appears cool but it never fit. As I get older I am learning to love myself even more for being me.

It takes courage to live a life that some people may not agree with but as long as you're happy who cares. Sometimes in this journey of discovery you lose some people along the way who have tried to put you in a box and that's okay. People will always come and go in your life and for good reason. Just because a person has been in your life doesn't mean that they should stay. People grow and change and that's just part of life.

Regardless if people accept you or not continue to be you and move forward to bigger and better things. Along your journey you will discover people who appreciate where you've been and where you're going.

Sasha always stood out since she was a little girl. When she got to high school she realized that standing out made a lot of people uncomfortable and judgmental. She was tall and skinny, had short blue hair, and dressed like she was from the 80's. She had a carefree spirit but that did not matter because the kids at school thought she was a freak. She did not fit in with a lot of people but could always count on her best friends Scott and Ashley. Even though people talked about Sasha behind her back she was always nice until she met this girl named Evelyn. Evelyn went out of her way to attack Sasha on a regular basis.

One day when Sasha was waiting in line for her lunch Evelyn bumped into her on purpose and spilled her food all over her clothes. The next day after that in gym class Evelyn threw a basketball at her face when she wasn't looking and broke Sasha's nose. Sasha was furious and asked Evelyn what her problem was. Evelyn said, "I just don't like you, you walk around here looking crazy and think nobody is supposed to say anything to you." Sasha replied, "Why do you care how I look I'm minding my own business and have you taken a look in the mirror lately." Evelyn walked away but it would not be the last time that the two would get into it. When Sasha got home she went straight to her room and cried. She could not imagine going through this every day and decided that this had to stop.

At school the next day she decided to talk to the principle about putting together a program for kids that were "so called" different. The principal liked the idea and told her to organize the group and to get other students involved. When Evelyn got wind of it she made sure that anyone who joined the group caught hell from her and her friends. At one of Sasha's meetings all of the members decided that enough was enough. They devised a perfect plan to show who Evelyn really was at a pep rally the next week. Without Evelyn knowing the kids in Sasha's group videotaped her hateful words, bullying, and pranks that she pulled that week.

During the middle of the pep rally Sasha got up in front of the whole school and played the videos from that week. The whole gym was quiet and Sasha began to speak.

"Since I have been coming to this high school Evelyn has made my life a living hell all because I am different. So what I have blue hair and my clothes are different. How does that make me a loser or a freak? I am a person just like you and deserved to be treated like one. How would she feel if I woke up one morning and decided to treat her the same way? Well thank God that I'm different because if I have to be like Evelyn to fit in I would die." Everyone started laughing! After her speech Evelyn and her friends rushed out of the gym while the crowd cheered Sasha on. From that day on Evelyn never messed with Sasha or anyone else for that matter again.

Everyone has different things that they love about themselves but what I want to know is how you treat others who are different from you? I know in high school there are so many cliques and the reason for that is because of different personalities, lifestyles, and differences. Just because someone does not act, look, or talk like you that doesn't mean that they are less than you or that you are better. Take the time out to get to know people before you judge them because you never know what you may have in common or how cool they really are.

It is vital that you learn to love everything about yourself because you are **UNIQUE** and everything else all wrapped up into one beautiful creation. Why would God make us all so different if we are supposed to be the same? That is why I encourage you to be yourself because we are all made different. Just because some people don't think the same thing about you does not mean that you are weird or a freak. If we were all the same it would really be boring. So whatever flavor you bring to the table make sure it's your own.

Everyone is not going to like you and that is okay. As long as you're keeping it real with yourself forget about everybody else. My mom would always remind me to watch how I carry myself. What she meant by that was if you act like a hoe you will get treated like one. If you act stupid people will treat you like you're stupid. If you carry yourself in a proper manner you will get respect because you respect yourself.

Be careful of what you see in magazines and watch on television. A lot of pictures are airbrushed and some actresses and actors go through a lot to look the way that they do. What you see in the mirror may not reflect what someone else sees and so what. I have met a lot of beautiful people who had ugly attitudes which made them really unattractive.

What really matters is that if you are beautiful on the inside it will reflect on the outside. I am not trying to be corny but it's true. I remember when I was in junior high and high school I went out with guys who most girls would not give a second look. When I dated someone the most important thing that mattered was the type of person they were not how they looked. Having that attitude paid off in the end because I have the most handsome and amazing husband.

If you have been blessed with a certain talent or skill do not let anyone stop you. If people do not want you to be yourself and love you for who you are forget them. You are great and will be great at whatever you do. The fact that you made this far in the book says a great deal about you or your parents for making you read it!

List 5 Things you LOVE about yourself

1.

2.

3.

4.

5.

List 5 Things you DISLIKE about yourself

1.

2.

3.

4.

5.

The good thing about having qualities that you dislike about yourself is that you can change them. I hate the way that I always interrupt people when I am trying to get my point across. Though I still do it especially when I'm mad I'm more conscious of it which helps because I can remind myself to be quiet and listen. It is going to take time but remember it is a process and to take it one day at a time. Remind yourself of the things you love about yourself when you do something to hurt yourself or someone else. You do have good qualities but always work on the bad ones.

What sets you apart from others?

_____

_____

_____

_____

_____

At some point everyone has felt lonely even in a room full of people. Loneliness can lead some to depression and other harmful behaviors. To ensure that it does not go that far I want you to know that you are **IMPORTANT**, you have a **PURPOSE**, and you have a **VOICE**. Appreciate being different and treat others who are different with respect. If you can remember this you will go really far in life because you acknowledge that people bring valuable things to the table because of their differences.

Ways to Help with Loneliness

- Reach out to someone you can trust

- Depend on someone or something greater than yourself

- Admit it to yourself and try to find ways to change it

- Find a good support system

INVISIBLE

I walk through the halls and no one even knows my name
And every day I wake up I think something's going to change
But when I walk through the school doors I am quickly reminded that some things
will always stay the same

I am not invisible
Well invisible to most people who look past my small frame, stringy hair, big feet,
and big eyes

My parents tell me how great I am and not to worry about what people say
It's easy for adults to make these types of comments
But if they were me they would go through hell everyday

I have seen more lockers than my books
And all of my lunch money goes to crooks who take it as they please

One day somebody will notice me and maybe even smile

Am I asking too much because all I want is for people to know that I exist
I am not just a student on my teacher's roster list

I like video games, music, having fun, but most of all I like being noticed,
recognized, seen, heard, acknowledged, and loved

Maybe one day when I wake up it will finally change and everyone will know my name

Who am I kidding that will never happen unless I turn into someone else
And I don't think that is possible because I would rather be invisible if I can't be
myself

Fall

October
Circumstances

"You don't have to stay where you are"

When you hear people talking about faith sometimes it goes through one ear and out the other. But it is important if you want to succeed in this life. In most situations you have faith already and you don't even realize it. You may have faith that:

- If you study you will get a decent grade

- When you use your GPS it will lead you in the right direction

- If you pray God will answer your prayers

You get the point right? Faith requires action on your part because you believe in something (God, Allah, Buddha, etc.) to get whatever you need accomplished. When you pursue something even though you do not know how it's going to work out that's faith. When you see great results that come from having faith it becomes easier to have it every day. Sometimes things you may want may seem like it is taking forever but be patient and keep the faith. Sometimes that is all you have to hold on too.

When was the last time you stepped out on faith?

_____

_____

_____

_____

Who do you put your faith in and why?

_____

_____

_____

_____

A lot of times when you look around you see people who do not want to change and are comfortable with being homeless, on welfare, drop-outs, addicts, etc. Just because you have been brought up in a certain environment does not mean that you have the same destiny that they do. If you want something better for yourself it is up to you to get it. Regardless of what limitations you may have or what others place on you remember there is no limit to what God can do. The only person who can stop you from being great is YOURSELF.

LIMITS

- You're so stupid I don't even know why you go to school

- You're just like your daddy/mama

- No wonder nobody wants you all you do is eat

- The only thing you will be good at is laying on your back

- I hate you

If this is what you are told on a constant basis I can understand why you are frustrated but know that is someone else's opinion. Usually, when people make comments like that they have nothing going for themselves so it is easier to tear someone else down. I have learned over the years that "hurt people hurt people".

Sidney grew up with her mama and two younger sisters Mimi and Tasha. They did not have much but there mama did the best she could. Since Sidney was a little girl her mother had men in and out the house to help pay the rent. Her mother did not care if the men looked at her daughters and would often ask if they wanted to make some extra money. When Sidney realized her mother didn't care she stayed away from home as much as possible. She was a good student and made excellent grades. She was always on the honor roll but stayed in the latest drama. Sidney was about 5 "9" slim but had curves in all the right places, smooth brown skin, green eyes, and long curly hair. The girls were jealous of her because she was beautiful and always had the best looking dude in school. Sidney knew how to make heads turn when she walked in a room but did not know how much power she held inside of her. She was 16 and you couldn't tell her nothing. Danielle and Tisha were her best friends and they did everything together. They had been hanging tight ever since grammar school and nobody could come between them. They all were as equally beautiful as Sidney so there was never any jealousy. All of them knew they all had what it took to pull the best. Sidney never had a problem keeping a boyfriend but each and every one of them treated her like a dog. She kept them around because she knew there was always a girl lined up to take them. She did not let them go until she had found someone else. Will was her first boyfriend, first love, and her first everything. Sidney always kept him close because she knew she would really need him one day. Little did she know she would need him sooner than she thought!

Sidney barely came home when anyone was there because she wanted to avoid her mother and her mother's men. This particular day she had nowhere to go so she decided to go home and chill in her room. As she was doing her homework she heard a knock on her bedroom door and ignored it. Bill one of her mom's regulars opened the door and said someone was at the door and that her mom went to the store. She could feel he was lying but did not want to be stuck in the room with him and would rather be close to the front door just in case he tried something. Sidney went to the door and it was her neighbor asking for money that her mama owed. Sidney was annoyed and slammed the door in their face. Bill started laughing and told her, "You is crazy just like yo mama". As Sidney walked passed he grabbed her butt and started smiling. When she turned around ready to throw down he punched her in the mouth. She tasted the blood as it slowly dripped into her mouth and could feel her heart pumping through her chest. As she tried to go out the door he grabbed her by the arm and punched her in the face again and said, "You ain't going nowhere without giving me some of that." Sidney knew what was about to happen and knew she could not stop him. He dragged her to her room and threw her on the bed. He grabbed her by the throat and then pushed her face down. He unzipped his pants and slid inside of her. She was screaming and he started to choke her until she stopped. She cried as he pushed himself further inside of her. After he was done he made her take a shower while he watched. After she was done he told her that if she ever told anyone he would kill her and her family. Sidney was not trying to hear that and as soon as he left the house she called her mama to tell her what happened. There was a silence on the phone until she heard her mom say, "Get out of my house! I always knew you would try something like this. That is what you get for trying to look cute around the house anyway. If you wanted some money you should have asked." As the phone went silent and with the receiver still up to Sidney's ear she sat there in silence and the let out a loud cry. She had nowhere to go and didn't want anyone to know what happened but knew one person she could always count on Danielle. She did not tell a soul what happened she figured if her mama didn't care then who did.

The next day she waited across the street until she knew the coast was clear and went into her house to get her stuff. As she was heading towards the door her anger started to build up and she went into her mother's room and trashed it. She ripped up all of her pictures, sheets, and took her money from her secret hiding spot. She knew her mama would be looking for her but she was ready for the war. She closed the door and did not look back because she knew she would never step foot in that house again.

After a couple of months of staying over her friend's house she found out that she was pregnant and immediately began to cry because she knew who the father was. Even though Sidney kept the best looking dudes she was not putting out like the rest because she did not want to end up like her mama. She had sex with her ex-boyfriend Will and a couple weeks later told him that she was pregnant and did not want to keep it. Will was glad that they were on the same page and gave her the money to go and take care of business. As she arrived at the abortion clinic she started to have doubts but knew that she could not take care of a child. "Sidney" the nurse called her name but she could not move. As she got up she felt like her feet were made of cement as her steps got slower and slower. When she walked into the room she felt her stomach drop and was unsure about going through with it. As she lay on the table she thought about the sex of the baby and how she always wanted a girl when she grew up. Tears started roll down her face as the procedure was about to begin. She knew from that moment on that she would not be the same.

As Sidney walked through those doors and back into reality she knew that she wanted revenge for what happened to her. A couple of days later when Sidney went to the store to get something to eat she spotted her mother. They both just stared at each other with disgust but did not say a word. Her mother turned her head and left without even acknowledging that Sidney existed. Sidney thought being raped was the worst feeling but nothing hurt her more than being disowned by her own mother. Sidney quickly wiped away a tear and got herself together.

She had no money, no job, no home, and could not go back to living with her friends. She knew how to make money quick because she watched her mom do it all her life and felt like she had no other way. She called one of her mom's old tricks who had their eye on her for a while and asked him if he had some cash. He quickly replied, "Yea, I always got a little something for you" and told her to meet him at the nearest motel. As Sidney sat there anxiously awaiting his arrival she began to have second thoughts. As soon as she grabbed her purse to leave there was a knock at the door. When she opened the door she saw a tall, skinny, greasy man who looked like he had not taken a shower in months and had not brushed his teeth in years. He wasn't the best looking thing but he had the money so she decided to make it. As he took off her clothes and started to kiss her she immediately got nauseous and started to sweat. While she laid there she remembered when she was little how she loved reading books to get away from everything and how her mama would put her hair in long pretty ponytails every night before she went to bed. She imagined she was in a different place until it was over. As he got off her to get dressed he gave her a $100 and left as quickly as he arrived. She looked at that money as if it loved her more than anybody else and realized she wanted more of it.

Over the next few months she built up her clientele and made more money than she imagined. Sidney put up with it even though it cost her more than she was willing to pay. It filled her void for a while but then she started feeling used up and all the money in the world could not erase that. She was still going to school and making good grades and still wanted to go to college. The only thing that held her back from her dreams was her mama's voice telling her she would never amount to anything. Sidney was always thinking about the college tour she took when she was 14 years old. She remembered how she felt being in an environment where it was normal to want to learn new things instead of being made fun of because you were smart. She knew right then and there that she wanted to do something different with her life.

Danielle and Tisha saw all the money Sidney was making and began to ask questions about how they could get down too. Sidney told them it was not what they wanted and they got really upset. Danielle replied, "You always thought you were cute with your long hair and green eyes. Don't nobody want to be a ho anyway that's your job." Tisha replied, "I know at least we don't have to spread our legs to get paid our looks are enough to get some dough." Sidney didn't think that her two best friends would ever talk to her like that but she was not surprised because deep down she knew they always envied her. "If that's how ya'll feel then don't say nothing else to me, keep it moving when you see me." The next day at school she was getting nasty looks from all the females and smiles from all the guys. Will walked up to her and asked her, "Is it true you out selling your *****." Sidney's eyes began to water as Will walked away in disgust but her tears soon dried as she saw Mimi and Tasha walking her way. They laughed at her and then threw money in her face as they walked by. Sidney knew that if she fought them she would have to fight everybody who made a comment about what she was doing but decided to take a different route. She held her head up high and concentrated on school. As months went by she was still selling her body to make ends meet but got enough credits to graduate school early. When she heard this news she got excited which quickly turned into anxiety because she knew she would need a parent's help to get into college. Her mother would die before helping her and only knew of one person who she could go to. Will's mom Ms. Marsh had always loved her even though Will and her were not together anymore. Sidney decided to call and set up a time to talk with her alone and Ms. Marsh agreed to meet that afternoon. She was nervous because she *would have to tell Ms. Marsh about the life she had been living but knew that she would not judge her because that was just the type of person she was. When Sidney arrived at Ms. Marsh's home she knocked quietly and put her head down. Ms. Marsh opened the door and knew that Sidney had a story to tell. Ms. Marsh replied, "Come in baby and tell me what has been going on and don't leave nothing out." Sidney explained everything and did not leave out any detail as much as it hurt. There was a silence for about 10 seconds which felt like 10 hours. God did not bring you this far to leave you and knew this day would come." Sidney did not understand why God would allow her to go through such horrible things if he really loved her. Ms. Marsh knew what Sidney was thinking and told her, "You will have a testimony that will help other girls just like you. God knows you are going to go through some tough things but he is with you through it all. I know you don't understand it but you will." Ms. Marsh told Sidney that God put it on her heart to help her get into college. Ms. Marsh prayed for her and tears began to stream down Sidney's face as she realized in that moment how much God really loved her. That night Sidney applied to Norfolk State University, Clark Atlanta University, and Howard University. She received acceptance letters and full scholarships from each one of them. Since her school was paid for she used the money she had saved while she was selling her body to put towards her little sister's education. She knew one day they would need it just like she did.*

Thought

There are millions of Sidney's out there waiting to be heard and loved. So many young girls choose to stay in that place of hurt because they cannot see anything beyond what is right in front of them. Well I am telling you that is not how it has to be. One thing that Sidney did was stay focused on one thing that was important which was education because she knew that lifestyle would not last and eventually lead to her death. As my pastor would say, "God uses ordinary people to do extraordinary things." Everyone is valuable to God even YOU. You may be reading this and think that your situation is not going to change but the change starts with you. If you want something different try God and see how far you will go. Sidney could have let her situation ruin her life but she wanted better for herself. God has faith in us but we have to say enough is enough.

Questions:

What could Sidney have done differently after she got raped?

_____

_____

_____

_____

Were Danielle and Tisha true friends? What is a true friend?

_____

_____

_____

_____

Why should you trust God?

_____

_____

_____

_____

What did you learn from Sidney's situation?

_____

_____

_____

_____

SURVIVING

Life has taught me so much in such a little time so I guess that makes me
wise
I have been through so much and conquered
But I do not think that I deserve a prize

My hardships have made me the person I am today and the only reason I can
stand proud is because someone taught me how to pray
And instilled in me that God will make a way out of no way

As I look around at the world and see how hate, greed, ignorance and
jealousy has destroyed so many lives
I am grateful that I was taught how to survive

Survive people who did not have my best interest at heart

Survive people who did not want to see me finish or make a fresh start

Survive jealousy by those I held close

Survive my denial that God did actually love me and discovering he was the
only one I needed to love me the most

Survive my mother's battle with learning how to love me

Survive my inner demons with sexuality while being in the dark and now I can
see

See that regardless of what I have been through every situation that I have
had I have come out
and as long as I keep living for the Lord I have no doubt

That I will continue to win not some of my battles but all of them

Be steadfast, unmovable, always abounding in the word and know who holds the rod
Remember you must keep the faith, be patient, and enjoy watching God be GOD

November
Word to the Wise

"Wisdom"

Josh was born and raised in Arkansas and he was proud of it. He grew up in a town that was predominantly White which meant that he did not have a lot of interaction with people of different races and cultures. All he knew about other cultures was what he saw on television and what people around him had taught him. Josh's dad got laid off from his factory job which meant that they had to do something quick because the rent would be due and they were already two months behind. They did not have much family there so they had no choice but to move. Josh and his family had to move to St. Louis, MO to live with his grandparents until his parents got back on their feet. Josh was in shock but what he saw all around him. He no longer lived in his bubble and felt like his life would soon end. He saw Blacks, Hispanics, and some Asian people all around his grandparent's neighborhood and immediately started to cry. His dad told him that he would be alright just don't speak to any of them.

When they arrived at the house Josh did not want to get out of the car. His grandpa asked, "Boy what's wrong with you ain't nobody gonna get you." Josh replied, "I know they have guns and probably sell all types of drugs around here." His grandpa replied, "You have been watching too much television boy this is nice neighborhood." Josh finally decided to get out of the car but not before checking his surroundings. He made sure that he was close to his father. When Josh got in the house he told his grandparents that he did not want to live by niggers and spics. His grandma just looked at him with sadness and told him, "that is exactly why they left." Josh was confused by his grandma's comment and didn't understand what she meant. "What do

113

you mean grandma?" The grandma replied, "People who think like that are very ignorant because they do not know any better but when you experience life and open your mind you realize there is more to life than color. I got tired of watching people get mistreated because they were different. They are people just like you Josh and you have to think about how would you feel if people didn't like you because of your skin color? They didn't ask to be born that way that is how God made them. Just because you see horrible things in the news does not mean that it applies to the whole race."

Josh was so upset by his grandma's comments because he felt like she was a trader and had been brain washed because she moved to Missouri. His parents did not say anything because they felt the same way. One day when Josh was sitting on his front porch a couple of kids walked up to him and asked if he wanted to play ball. He sat there and ignored them but desperately wanted to make new friends. He was surprised to see all the kids playing together Black, White, Hispanic, etc. but was not going to get sucked in like his grandparents.

After months of being by himself he decided to take a chance and go play ball with the guys on his block. He had never had so much fun in his life and continued to play every day. When he got home one evening his father asked him if you he enjoyed playing ball with his nigger friends. Josh responded, "Please, I just needed something to do. I'm tired of sitting around here all day." Inside Josh felt like crap because they were the total opposite of what he was taught. He knew his father would not understand so he just kept quiet and continued to talk bad about them.

Josh told his grandma about his new feelings and asked her why his parents hated people so much. She simply said, "Sweetie it's because they hate themselves. How can you not like *someone you have never met? When you hate a whole race just because they are different that is just pure ignorance. This world is too big and life is too short to waste it with thoughts like that."*

Our minds can think of some crazy things and play tricks on us if we are not careful. You have to be conscious of what and who you let in there. It is so important that you have an open mind and question any and everything. One of the worst things that can happen to a person is having a closed mind. People who are racist, homophobic, overly religious, etc. are people who have closed minds. They do not listen to any other ideas accept their own or they are stuck on what they have been taught to guide them. They are so stuck on their way of thinking that they are right and you are wrong. If God is love why do we hate one another? This is the type of question that you should be asking yourself.

What you watch and who you listen to can affect you in many ways. Subconsciously what you listen to or watch influences you without you even realizing it. For example, if I watch a show like Bad Girls Club I might start picking up bad habits or thinking that what they do on the show is cool. If you are constantly listening to them cuss each other out and fight you may pick some up some of their bad habits and not even realize it. It is important to evaluate what and who is influencing you because once again what you allow in will come out.

What do you listen to that may you may need to change?

_____

_____

_____

_____

What television shows do you watch that you may need to turn off?

_____

_____

_____

_____

Growing up I always thought that my parents were trying to ruin my life. I was the girl who was always grounded because I came in late, had a bad grade, or just did something I wasn't supposed to. Believe it or not I was not allowed to watch television on the weekdays and had to make sure my chores and homework were done before I went outside (I know). When I look back at why my mom punished me it all makes sense today. She was trying to instill great things in me and wanted me to become a productive adult. Because of my mom as an adult I have made a lot of great decisions because of the way I was brought up. I am not saying that life has been perfect but I have avoided a great deal of misery and pain because of such a strong woman in my life.

If you think your parents have some crazy rules that you think are ruining your social life know that they love you and just want to protect you from making some bad choices. I know they cannot protect you from everything because you will make your own choices but I challenge you to just **LISTEN**. Your parents were teenagers once too believe it or not so they know what you are going through. It is true that times have changed but the struggles are still the same.

Sometimes it seems as though your parents just want to destroy your social life but if you look long and hard what would your life look like without rules or boundaries? Do your parents love you more if they allow you to do anything you want to do? Absolutely not, it means that they do not care as much as they should or that they do not know any better. For example, say you came home drunk one night and your parents were like your grounded but you could still do everything you wanted the next day. So you decided to get drunk again and the same thing happened. The next time you decided to drink you got a DUI or worse died from an accident. This could have all been prevented if you were disciplined the first time and realized that there are consequences for your actions. Even when you grow up you still have rules (speed limits, you have to pay taxes, pay bills, etc.). I know it sucks but hey that's life.

What are some of the things that your parents get on you for?

_____

_____

_____

_____

_____

_____

Why do you think that is?

_____

_____

_____

_____

_____

_____

_____

If you truly feel like your parents do not understand you sometimes it is best that you sit down with them and explain why you feel the way that you do. I remember when I was not allowed to date before the age of 16 and I got caught having a boyfriend. I pleaded my case and I told my mom that I really, really, really liked this boy and she said it was okay. Of course there were a lot of rules but she compromised with me. I'm not saying that they will always say yes but it is worth a try.

SHOULDA, COULDA, WOULDA

I should have listened to you when you told me not to grow up so fast

I should have done a lot of things

I wish those words would have stayed in my heart instead of in the air

I don't understand why it takes so long for me to get it
I promise you I want to do better
I know I have made this statement before and sometimes my actions change just
like the weather

I don't want to be last anymore I want to be first

I want to reach the next level and live up to my full potential

I want to do a lot of things but I know I have to open up my ears
Because of my actions I have wasted a lot of years

Running with my friends and staying out all night
Constantly getting into trouble over little things that didn't matter and always
getting into fights

Smoking all the time and skipping all my classes at school
I thought I could make up that time
I thought I was being cool

I should have listened when you told me not to grow up so fast

I could have really been somebody great
Little did I know that death would be my fate

I was always the life of the party especially when I had a few drinks
My friends never stopped me from drowning they always let me sink

They let me drive home drunk because I have done it a thousand times before

I told them this time was different but all they did was ignore me

I knew I had to get home so I grabbed my keys and left
Because at the end of the day the only person I could count on was myself

At first I was doing fine but the liquor took over mind
I saw the lights flashing but I could not move my car out of the way in time

My head was throbbing so bad all I could think of was what you said
That if I didn't slow down soon I was going to end up dead

I should have listened to you when you told me not to grow up so fast

December
Sex

"Everybody's doing it"

Sex is not just physical but it is emotional and mental too. A lot of times once you give it up to a certain someone they go elsewhere because that is all they want or either they stay because they can get it whenever they want to. Then you are left feeling guilty, used up, angry, etc. **Remember once you give it away you can never get it back!** Some kids are so quick to give it up because they think they are in love but in reality when you have sex everything changes. If you are not comfortable and you are not ready to accept the consequences that come with sex you shouldn't be doing it.

Having sex is a big decision that can change your whole life and it may be something that you regret as well. If you are not informed properly about sex it can lead to STD's, pregnancy, bad reputation, hurt family members, and so on.

How to Avoid Sex

- Always date in groups
- Remember the risks
- Don't put yourself in any situation where you two are alone
- Try to limit physical contact
- Have people hold you accountable

Is there a lot of pressure to have sex in your school?

_____

_____

_____

_____

How do you feel about sex?

_____

_____

_____

_____

With shows like 16 & Pregnant and Teen Mom one would think that young women and men would see the cons to having a child at such a young age. I am concerned when I see so many young people having babies and can barely take care of themselves. There are some exceptions but there are very few. The one that suffers the most is the child because they didn't ask to be here. You cannot be selfish anymore it is all about that child or children. If you have not finished high school or are a drop out what kind of life can you provide especially if you are a single parent and do not have any help?

Love doesn't allow you to keep having babies when you and I know you cannot handle the one(s) that you have already. Is it fair to your child for you to bring them into a world with no father or mother and with the weight of the world on their shoulders? Now they are left with the responsibility of making you feel loved because you are alone. Or is it fair to have different men/women in and out of their lives because of your selfish desire or low self-esteem. I'm not trying to be mean but I want to help you realize that your choices not only affect you but those

around you as well.

NEW BEGINNING

A new life has begun and a seed has begun to grow
My flower is blossoming and it is really beginning to show

The reflection in the mirror which is me
I am proud to look up and see all that I have grown up to be

I can honestly look back and say I would do it all over again
Because regardless I would still pass the finish line and win

Every day is a new day which means a fresh start
And the people that I take for granted will always stay close to my heart

Coming a long way means you've been somewhere
And now that my present is facing me I am no longer scared

Of the things that I once was afraid of like rejection, love, and pain
But now I know that all of those things were just something to gain so I could
experience each one so I could taste a little bit of life

Knowing there would be disappointments to keep me down and full of hurt
I never let them get the best of me because I always knew what I was worth

You Made It!!!

Well you made it to the end and I hope you got through the book without getting slapped by your parents or friends for telling them how you really feel. I hope that you take only what applies to you and use to grow and to continue to blossom into something beautiful. I know sometimes the world views young people today as a lost cause but you are just misunderstood. Take time to understand the world a little better, listen to your parent's wisdom, follow people who are headed in the right direction, cut the people out who take away from your life, and remember that the choices you make will always have good or bad consequences.

"Always remember you cannot change people because they have to want that for themselves but you can change YOU!"

Letter to the Young Ladies,

How you carry yourself speaks volumes and know that just being pretty or fine will not last. At the end of the day you are going to need more than that to get through this life. Looks will fade but if you have some common sense, wisdom, education, and much more you will get somewhere. I'm not perfect nor do I try to be but I can't go on one more day without sharing my thoughts with you. I know many will read this and not give it a second thought but imagine how powerful this would be if you took a deep look at your life and evaluated some things.

You have to love yourself first before you invite someone into your world. You can tell if you love yourself by looking at your relationships and who you surround yourself with. At the end of the day you have to be accountable for yourself and hold yourself responsible for the choices that you make. I have been there so I know what not loving yourself can lead into and trust me it's not pretty. You allow men to use you in exchange for sex, nice clothes, money, etc.

I have heard this too many times "I can do what I want to do; I don't care what no one else thinks". Well that's a sad mentality to have because you should care what your family thinks of you. People do look up to you believe it or not. I have young cousins and I think about them and how they would feel because I don't want them to make the same mistakes and I want better for them. Enjoy being young and don't grow up too fast!

Love,

Kerra

Letter to the Young Men,

There are so many kids wandering around without fathers/mothers or with fathers/mothers who do not set a good example. There are so many misguided young men selling drugs, not working, not going to school or graduating, etc. There are a lot of men doing the exact opposite so I know it is possible to be something great.

I know a lot of men who choose the life of drugs and it always ends the same way. My heart is so heavy because their families are the ones that suffer the most. I know everyone makes mistakes but when it becomes a continuous thing that's when it's a problem. How do you expect people to respect you if you keep going in and out of the system?

You have to be accountable and own up to the mistakes you have made and remember that it is not too late to change or fix what has been broken. We all want what to enjoy this life that is sometimes too short so let's make that change. I have hope that soon young men will see that their leadership is needed and valued. I know that some of you know that what you are doing is wrong but have no clue as to how to fix the problem. Well it is simple; it starts with yourself and admitting that some things need to change. You need a higher power (God) to guide you and some strong men who are good examples to lead the way. Surround yourself with people who want something better out of life and are going somewhere. I know you have been friends with the same people for forever but you can't take everyone along with you on your journey. I could go on and on but I think you get the point that I am trying to make. You make your own choices just remember they have consequences!

Love,

Kerra

About the author

My name is Kerra Williams and I live in Illinois with my husband Tommy and our dog Boss. My hometown is Columbia, MO but I grew up all over because my mom was in the military. I am what some would call a military brat. I graduated from the University of Missouri with a Bachelors in Psychology and received my Master's degree in Counseling Psychology at Capella University. I have been working with children and teens since 2006. Working with kids and their families has allowed me to see the world in a different light and understand the responsibility that I have to them. It is important to me that families stick together and learn how to communicate their issues. My purpose has been clear since I was a little girl and that was to help people any way that I can and to always be the change I want to see.

Website: www.kerrascomfort.com

Contact me by email: looking4change@kerrascomfort.com

Contact me by mail:
Kerra's Comfort
P.O. Box 474
Decatur, IL 62525